# PHP Development with Windows Subsystem for Linux (WSL)

by Joe Ferguson

a php[architect] guide

## PHP Development with Windows Subsystem for Linux (WSL)

php[architect] edition published: December 2020

| | |
|---|---|
| Print ISBN: | 978-1-940111-90-2 |
| PDF ISBN: | 978-1-940111-87-2 |
| ePub ISBN: | 978-1-940111-88-9 |
| Mobi ISBN | 978-1-940111-89-6 |

Produced & Printed in the United States

### Disclaimer

**Written by**
Joe Ferguson

**Managing Editor**
Oscar Merida

**Editor**
Kara Ferguson

**Layout**
Oscar Merida

**Published by**
musketeers.me, LLC.
4627 University Dr
Fairfax, VA 22030 USA

240-348-5PHP (240-348-5747)
info@phparch.com
www.phparch.com

# Table of Contents

# About the Author

Joe Ferguson is a software developer, open source geek, and community organizer. He is involved with many different technology related initiatives including Memphis Technology Foundation and Open Sourcing Mental Illness LTD. He's been married to his extremely supportive and amazing wife for a really long time and she turned him into a crazy cat man. They live in the Memphis suburbs with their two cats. @JoePFerguson

# Chapter

# 1

# PHP Development With Windows Subsystem for Linux

Does a recent announcement by Microsoft have you wondering how you'll continue to use Windows for PHP development? Anyone with a compiler and the PHP source code should be able to build a PHP executable for Windows. If the thought of compiling your PHP binary on Windows seems daunting, have no fear! We're going to install native Ubuntu PHP packages on Windows!

On July 9th, 2020, a Service Engineer with Microsoft who has been working with the PHP internals team on Windows PHP builds announced Microsoft would no longer be providing builds for PHP 8.0. You can read the full email via externals.io[1]. There's another followup statement on PHP[2] which assures the community that:

> *"While we will no longer work on PHP builds for Windows, expect to see us remain involved in PHP in many ways across MS as we continue supporting PHP developers and collaborating with the community on security fixes."*

While many readers may think, "LOL, WINDOZE!" Microsoft has always been very good to the PHP community and ecosystem. Microsoft has long maintained and hosted Windows builds of PHP binaries. This work has been an excellent service, but with native PHP on Windows going away after 7.4, what's the solution? Are we unable to develop on Windows?!

Don't Panic! You'll still be able to run PHP 7.4 and lower on Windows as long as they're supported; active support ends on November 28th, 2021, while security support remains until November 28th, 2022. You can always see the current PHP support timelines on php.net[3]. What about running PHP 8 and beyond? How are we supposed to continue developing with PHP? Anyone with a compiler and the PHP source code should be able to build a PHP executable for Windows.

The better alternative to running PHP on Windows is to run PHP on Linux on Windows. Does this sound impractical? Read on to see what Microsoft has been working on!

## What Is WSL?

Windows Subsystem for Linux[4] (WSL) is a set of components running on Windows 10 allowing the operating system to run native Linux ELF64 binaries. The TL;DR explanation is, "What was compiled on 64 bit Linux can run." You can find the more in-depth and quite over my head explanation can on WikiPedia about the ELF Format[5]. These components involve:

- a user-mode session manager to handle the Linux instance lifecycle,
- Pico providers which are drivers to emulate the Linux kernel by translating the system calls,

---

[1]  externals.io: https://externals.io/message/110907
[2]  statement on PHP: https://externals.io/message/110985
[3]  php.net: https://www.php.net/supported-versions.php
[4]  Windows Subsystem for Linux: https://docs.microsoft.com/en-us/windows/wsl/
[5]  ELF Format: https://phpa.me/wikip-elf-format

- and Pico processes hosting the unmodified binaries (such as /bin/bash).

You can't install and run desktop environments such as Gnome or KDE. However, all of the command line tools macOS users typically install via Homebrew[6] can be installed as if you were running Ubuntu natively on your machine. Think of WSL as a replacement for Homebrew on Windows, but better because you're not running macOS binaries—you're running the same binaries as you would on a production Ubuntu server. This includes PHP, Composer, Apache, NGINX, Ruby, MongoDB, and on and on. As far as the Linux programs can tell, they're running in a Linux environment.

To follow along, you should ensure you're running Windows 10 Build 18945 or newer. If not, upgrade to the latest Windows version or contact your IT administrators to facilitate your upgrade if a corporate IT team manages the machine.

## WSL 2

WSL 2 was recently released and is still rolling out to Windows 10 users. If you're not already running Windows 10 2004, search for "Windows Update" in the settings application, and you should see an option about upgrading to version 2004. This version is the minimum required for WSL 2, which is what we're using throughout. The main improvements included are a full Linux kernel. WSL 1 previously only virtualized parts of the Linux kernel, limiting what you were able to do and run in WSL. While file performance was another area of vast improvement, it is still the most noticeable bottleneck. The WSL team has stated they're aware and working on an upcoming release to address the slow file performance/high latency you may see. Under the hood, WSL runs in a Hyper-V virtual machine, and your WSL filesystem is accessed as a mapped network drive. Windows takes care of mapping and mounting this drive in Explorer for you automatically. If you're curious about the differences between versions, there's a useful chart in the documentation to compare versions[7].

> *Hyper-V is a virtualization hypervisor provided by Microsoft. It allows users to run virtual machines or use the hypervisor as a provider for Vagrant. If you're still using Virtualbox, I highly recommend looking into Hyper-V as the performance is much better in my experience.*

---

[6]  Homebrew: <u>https://brew.sh</u>
[7]  compare versions: <u>https://phpa.me/wsl-version</u>

The only time you should intentionally use WSL 1 is if your project files *must* be stored on Windows instead of the Linux operating system's drive, or if you need to cross-compile. Thankfully, most PHP applications shouldn't fall under this; we'll be using WSL 2 for our examples.

## What Is a WSL Distribution?

A WSL distribution is a fancy way of describing a Linux distribution which has been installed and customized into a ready-to-run state. Much like a Vagrant box or a VirtualMachine snapshot, the WSL distros don't need to be installed. The only set up the first time it runs is creating the Linux user account. If you search for "Linux" in the Microsoft Store app, you'll find Ubuntu, Kali Linux, Debian, and SUSE Linux among the options, as shown in Figure 1.1.

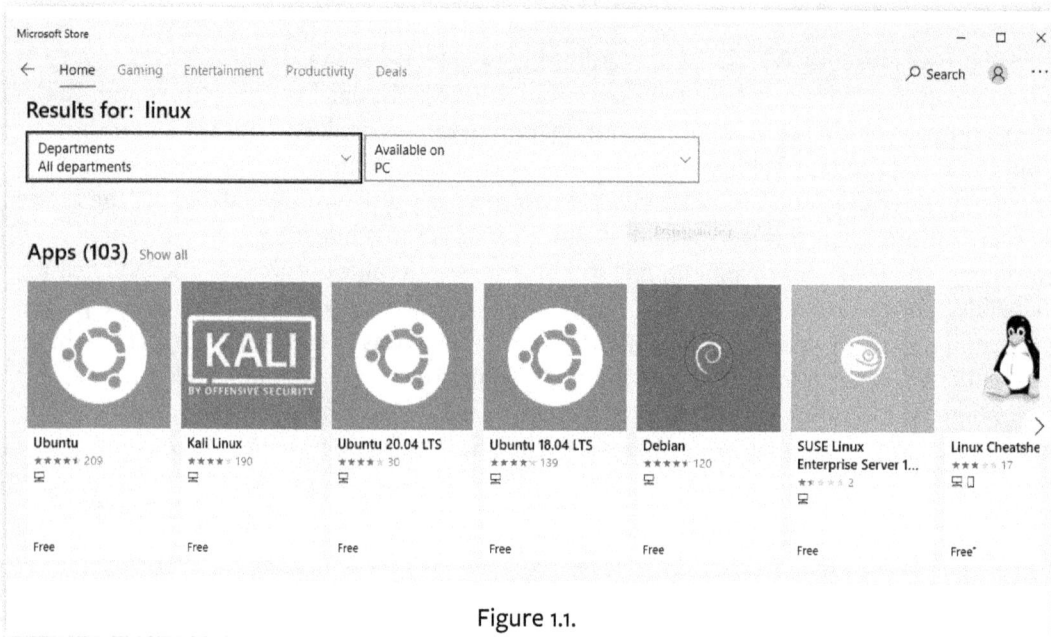

Figure 1.1.

# Installing WSL and Linux

Before installing a Linux distribution, we need to ensure we have the Windows Subsystem for Linux installed and enabled. We need to open the Control Panel and run "Windows Features." Scroll down to the bottom and ensure "Windows Subsystem for Linux" is checked (Figure 1.2).

If you didn't have the WSL feature enabled, you might need to reboot your computer before continuing.

To install Ubuntu, we need to open the Microsoft Store application, found by clicking on the Windows logo start button or by pressing the Windows logo key on your keyboard (usually located between the left "Ctrl" control key and the left "ALT" alternate key). I prefer to start typing to filter the results instead of hunting for things in the start menu. Once open, we need to search for "ubuntu," which returns Ubuntu, Ubuntu 18.04 LTS, and Ubuntu 20.04 LTS as in Figure 1.3. For this example, we're using Ubuntu 20.04, but this process should be quite similar on 18.04.

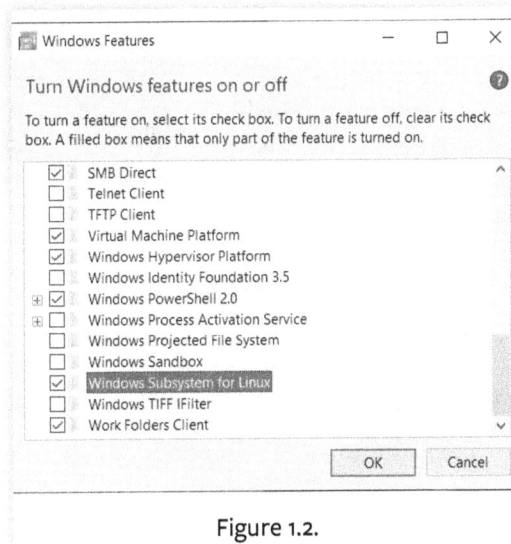

Figure 1.2.

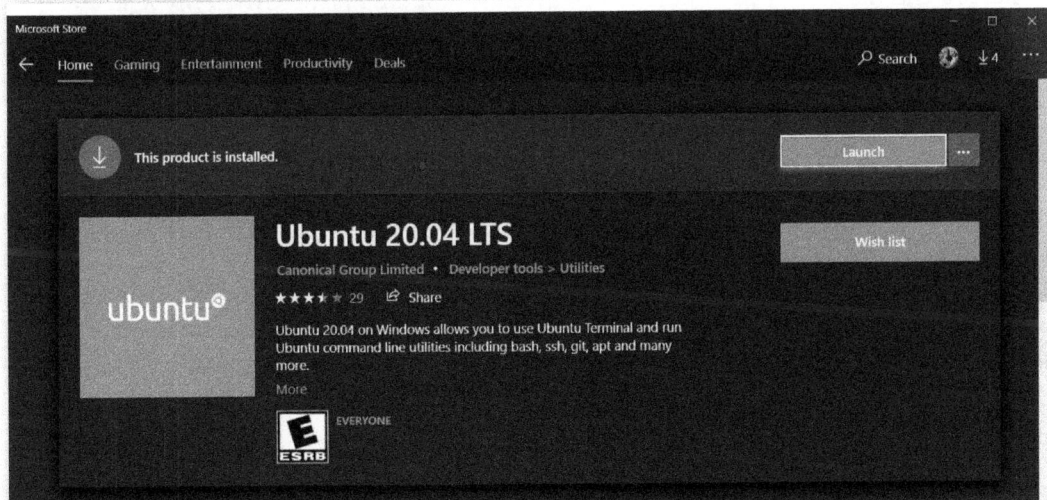

Figure 1.3.

A first-time installation of a WSL distro can take a few minutes depending on your hardware. This process is initializing the virtualized hard drive you'll be operating on. Hyper-V is taking care of all the virtualization requirements under the hood. You don't have to worry about booting the VM or installing the operating system. See Figure 1.4.

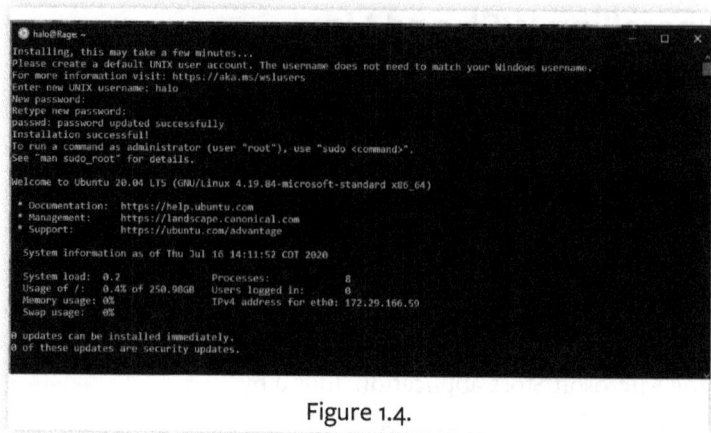

Figure 1.4.

When the installation is complete, we are greeted by the Ubuntu message of the day and a command prompt. Remember, the user account you created during this install is your *Linux* account, which does not have to match your Windows account.

The first thing we should do is update Ubuntu by running:

```
sudo apt-get update && sudo apt-get -y upgrade
```

This downloads and installs any updates released since our Ubuntu WSL distro was built.

The next step is a bit complicated, and I don't want to draw attention away from WSL, so here's a GitHub gist[8] you can use to install and configure PHP, NGINX, MySQL, and a handful of other tools into your WSL distro. Before running this script, you should search and replace halo, my username with your *Linux* username. If you skip this step, the installer fails.

We're about to run this script from the GitHub Gist, but before we do, you should ensure the script has Unix line endings, or Ubuntu won't know how to execute the script. You can do this in Jetbrains IDEs by going to File > Settings > Editor > Code Style > Line separator and selecting "Unix and macOS ()." Alternatively, could install dos2unix via `sudo apt-get install -y dos2unix` and run `dos2unix /path/to/script.sh` to convert the line endings automatically. I strongly recommend you set the line separator in your editor as I often forget to run `dos2unix`; you can safely skip this if your editor is already using \n.

---

[8]   GitHub gist: *https://phpa.me/svpernova09-bc441*

The script takes a few to several minutes, depending on your internet speed. Once complete, we can run php --version and see we have PHP 7.4.8 installed as in Figure 1.5.

Figure 1.5.

Don't forget to setup your Git user:

```
git config --global user.name "Your Name"
git config --global user.email "youremail@domain.com"`
```

*I also generate new SSH keys for this new user and add those to my GitHub/Gitlab/ version control sites. While this is out of the scope of WSL, you can create new keys with:*

```
ssh-keygen -t rsa
```

Next, we're going to install a new Laravel project with Composer:

```
composer create-project --prefer-dist laravel/laravel blog
```

We have created this new project in the WSL distro's hard drive. We can open the project in our editor by opening the folder Z:\home\halo\Code\blog, which is where Windows has mounted my WSL drive (Figure 1.6). It's important to remember never to edit Windows files in Linux. It's entirely possible to break things in possibly fun and interesting ways; I wouldn't want to debug what happens.

Opening our fresh Laravel application in PhpStorm shows these two notifications. One is a warning to allow you to configure (or let Jetbrains do it) Windows Defender to ignore/ allow operations in the project folder. The second notification is warning you file changes may be slow due to storing the files on a network mount.

This brings us to a common pain point in virtualization: File sharing is hard, slow, and annoying. It's hard because it's virtualization all the way down the rabbit hole, slow because you're virtualizing the files themselves, properties, and permissions across two operating systems at the same time. Just like VirtualBox shared folders are slow in Vagrant, these files *are* slow to be accessed, but it's not unreasonable. Your tolerances may not be as flexible as mine, but I encourage you to give this a test drive and see how you like it. Comparing a 2018 quad-core Hyperthreaded MacBook Pro with 16 GB of RAM running Vagrant and VirtualBox to my eight physical core 64GB of RAM desktop computer, I notice the file slow down. Still, everything else runs so fast it has seemed to make up for it. If possible, store your operating system on a Solid State Drive (SSD) for faster disk input/output performance. You don't have to buy a state-of-the-art, top of the line PC with monster components to test drive WSL; if you're already running Windows 10, you likely already have access to it.

We have configured WSL and created a Laravel application. Now, we need to create a Virtual Host for NGINX to use to serve our application via PHP-FPM, which was installed and configured by the install script earlier. You can use the `virtualhost.conf` from the previously used Gist as a template for your project; make sure to edit the root and error_log sections to your paths. I recommend you copy the virtual host file to your editor (configured to use Unix line endings), make your changes there, and then copy the contents of the file. Returning to our WSL distro window, we run the following to open a new file:

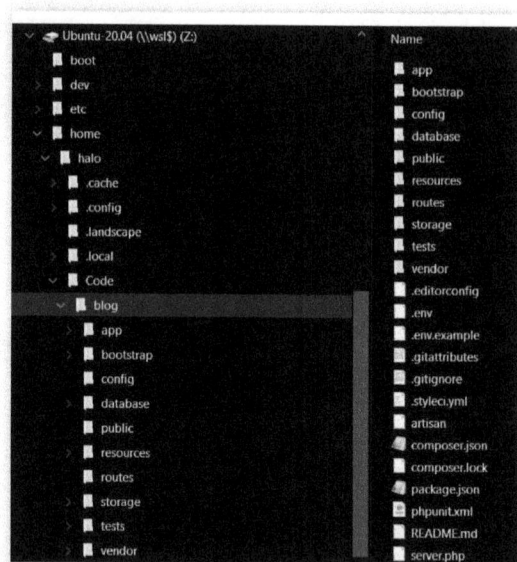

Figure 1.6.

```
sudo vi /etc/nginx/sites-enabled/laravel.test
```

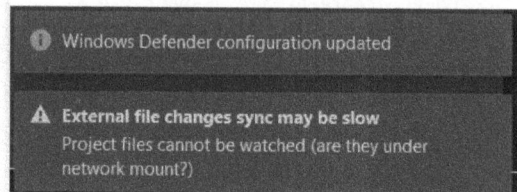

Figure 1.7.

Then, hit the i key to enter *insert* mode, then paste. Next, we hit escape and then :wq and "enter" to write the file and quit vim. Feel free to use Nano or any other preferred Linux text editor. Remember to *not* use a Windows application to edit Linux files, including your virtual hosts.

Once you have saved the virtual host file we're ready to restart services:

```
$ sudo service nginx restart
* Restarting nginx nginx [ OK ]
$ sudo service php7.4-fpm restart
* Restarting PHP 7.4 FastCGI Process Manager php-fpm7.4 [ OK ]
```

If one or both of those services don't restart properly, you likely have an issue with a path somewhere. I would double-check your paths to your code and the usernames you're using. Once restarted, we can open a browser in Windows and navigate to `http://localhost:80`. You should see something like Figure 1.8.

What about `http://laravel.test/`? Because there's no magical DNS happening, neither Windows nor WSL Ubuntu are aware that `laravel.test` is a domain we want to route to. To overcome this, we open Notepad as an administrator and open `C:\Windows\system32\drivers\etc\hosts`, then add the `127.0.0.1 laravel.test` to the end of the file. Save your changes and then load `http://laravel.test` in your browser, and it should load the same "Laravel" welcome screen we saw when viewing the localhost.

We need to connect to a database and our already installed script and configured MySQL 8.0 for use. The username is whatever username you put in the script (mine was `halo`), and the password is `secret`. We can also see via the MySQL CLI that we have a database named `halo` we can use for our application, see Figure 1.9.

Once we update our `/home/halo/Code/blog/.env` file with our proper database credentials, we can run our migrations as in Figure 1.10

Now we're ready to dive into building the next great application!

Figure 1.8.

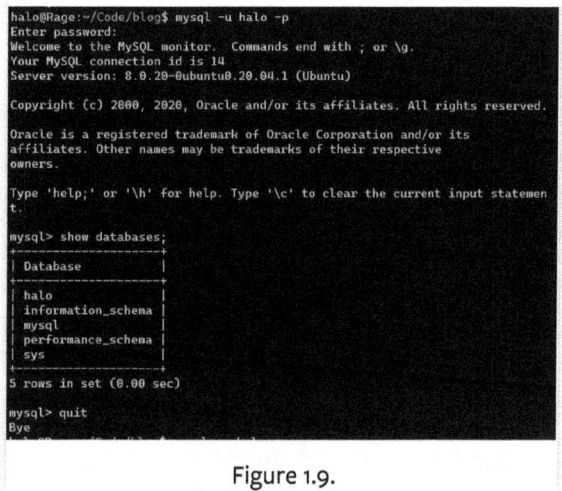

Figure 1.9.

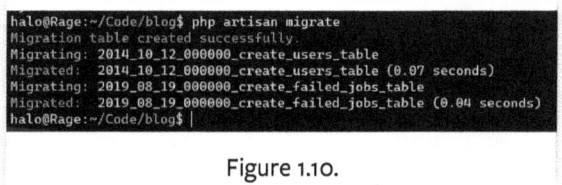

Figure 1.10.

WSL in the background runs Linux services and handles ports for you. Note that we didn't have to open port 80 for NGINX. WSL dealt with this for us and made it work transparently as if it was on our Windows localhost instead of where it's running, the Linux localhost. The same with MySQL and port 3306. You can use any SQL GUI you'd like; just connect to localhost.

If you're ready to be done with WSL or if you've broken something and need to reset everything, you can follow these commands to export your WSL Distro as an archived file, which you can restore later if you'd like. Then, we terminate the WSL distro, which "turns off" the underlying VM and finally unregister the distro, which removes it from the system. At this point, we can return to the Microsoft Store app and reinstall the same, or different distribution and start over with a clean slate. To learn more about the export/import process, check out the blog post I wrote Exporting and Importing WSL Linux Distributions on Windows 10[9].

Make sure you run these commands from a *Powershell* window and not the WSL distro.

```
wsl --export Ubuntu-20.04 Ubuntu-20.04.tar
wsl --terminate Ubuntu-20.04
wsl --unregister Ubuntu-20.04
```

PHP has long suffered the stigma of being the same scripting language everyone remembers from the 90s. PHP Developers should give Windows another shot, just like we tell other language developers to give PHP a chance because it's not your dad's PHP anymore. This new Microsoft has committed to open source, and being able to run Linux binaries alongside Windows binaries is a huge step for developer happiness. I hope you give Windows 10 a chance, at the time of this writing in mid-July 2020, I'm all in on Windows 10 only using my Macbook Pro if I'm away from the house or doing something macOS specific. I'd be hard-pressed to buy another Apple laptop in the future.

---

[9]  *Exporting and Importing WSL Linux Distributions on Windows 10: https://phpa.me/joeferguson-wsl-win10*

# Chapter

# 2

# Mail, Ngrok, and Xdebug in WSL

In the last chapter we covered Windows Subsystem for Linux and this month we're continuing the journey by demonstrating how to further work with our WSL distribution using tools such as Mailhog, Xdebug with PhpStorm and Visual Studio Code, and ngrok[1]

---

[1] ngrok: *https://ngrok.com*

# Mail Testing With MailHog

Email is one of the biggest pains I come across in local development. Frequently, I rely on at least a local mail relay to send mail and sometimes just plain ole SMTP server on the system. We can leverage WSL to install and configure a basic mail relay using Postfix to relay mail to MailHog[2], an email testing tool for developers. MailHog runs a local SMTP server that can be used by our application to send an email, but catch it before it leaves our system. Now *any* email the system generates will be handled by Postfix and relayed to MailHog. Since we're avoiding real email servers, we won't have to worry about accidentally sending out order confirmations to test email addresses, which may or may not be valid.

### Postfix Setup

While Postfix may sound unpleasant, we can easily skip much of the complexity by following the commands in Listing 2.1 to install Postfix in WSL and configure it to relay mail to the default MailHog IP and port (Which is `0.0.0.0` and `1025`).

Listing 2.1.

```
 1. # Install & Configure Postfix
 2. echo "postfix postfix/mailname string wsl.test" \
 3.   | debconf-set-selections
 4. echo "postfix postfix/main_mailer_type string 'Internet Site'" \
 5.   | debconf-set-selections
 6.
 7. apt-get install -y postfix
 8. sed -i "s/relayhost =/relayhost = [localhost]:1025/g" \
 9.   /etc/postfix/main.cf
10.
11. /etc/init.d/postfix reload
```

Installing postfix and configuring it like this routes all system mail through MailHog. An added bonus is that it also installs Postfix's Sendmail compatible binary, so `mail()`[3] will work and also send everything through MailHog. You get a robust way to ensure your applications aren't going to send an email out to real addresses, at least not without actively bypassing these defaults.

---

[2]  MailHog: https://github.com/mailhog/MailHog
[3]  `mail()`: https://php.net/mail

> *Feel free to skip the Postfix step. I always configure my Linux systems to route all mail to MailHog, but you won't miss much by not installing Postfix and using SMTP directly in your code.*

## Installing MailHog

To download and install the latest MailHog release we can run the following commands:

```
wget --quiet -O /usr/local/bin/mailhog \
  https://github.com/mailhog/MailHog/releases/download/v0.2.1/MailHog_linux_amd64
chmod +x /usr/local/bin/mailhog
```

Now we can run MailHog and send the process to the background via `mailhog >/dev/null&`. You should see output similar to Figure 2.1.

```
┌(~/LinuxCode/blog)(1:mailhog)
└ mailhog >/dev/null&
[1] 15623
2020/08/18 16:15:00 Using in-memory storage
2020/08/18 16:15:00 [SMTP] Binding to address: 0.0.0.0:1025
2020/08/18 16:15:00 Serving under http://0.0.0.0:8025/
```

Figure 2.1.

## Sending Email

Now that we have MailHog running, we need our demo blog application to send an email to our users when a new blog post is published. Laravel has fantastic tooling around creating and sending emails. However, our focus is on our application's email delivery handling. We'll use generic code in our email creation example, see Listing 2.2.

### Listing 2.2. app/Mail/NewBlogPublished.php

```
1. public function build() {
2.     $user = App\User::find(1); // get our specified user
3.     $post = App\Post::find(32); // get our latest blog post
4.
5.     return $this->view('email.new-blog-published')->with([
6.         'user' => $user,
7.         'url' => $post->url,
8.     ]);
9. }
```

We're retrieving information about our user who has opted into our new blog post email campaign. We get the post and pass these variables to our email template view, which is how we'll define our email output.

File resources/views/email/new-blog-published.blade.php is a few lines:

```
Hello {{ $user->name }},

We wanted to let you know a new blog has been
published at {{ $url }};
```

Before we run our code to send the email we created, we need to update our application configuration to send mail via MailHog. Laravel stores the mail settings in the application's .env file in the root of the project:

```
MAIL_MAILER=smtp
MAIL_HOST=localhost
MAIL_PORT=1025
MAIL_USERNAME=null
MAIL_PASSWORD=null
MAIL_ENCRYPTION=null
MAIL_FROM_ADDRESS=no-reply@domain.com
MAIL_FROM_NAME="${APP_NAME}"
```

We want our application to send an email via the SMTP protocol (which you can easily remember as *Send Mail To People*) on port 1025, the default MailHog port. We can also specify the "From:" address and name. We can skip the mail credentials because MailHog accepts anything there, including null. The next time we publish a blog post, our application triggers a new app/Mail/NewBlogPublished.php to users who have opted to receive notifications. I'm going to cheat and use the php artisan tinker command to trigger the email to send for testing:

*Transactional email providers usually provide an SMTP interface for sending messages, which you'd configure here. Often, you have a username and can generate one or more keys to use as passwords authentication. Use a unique key per app to revoke a key if one application misbehaves without affecting your other applications' email capabilities.*

When we run the Mail::to() method, the application logs the output of the SMTP connection with MailHog, as shown in Figure 2.2. With the email sent, we can open the MailHog user interface by browsing to http://localhost:8025 to see a new email from our application shown in Figure 2.3.

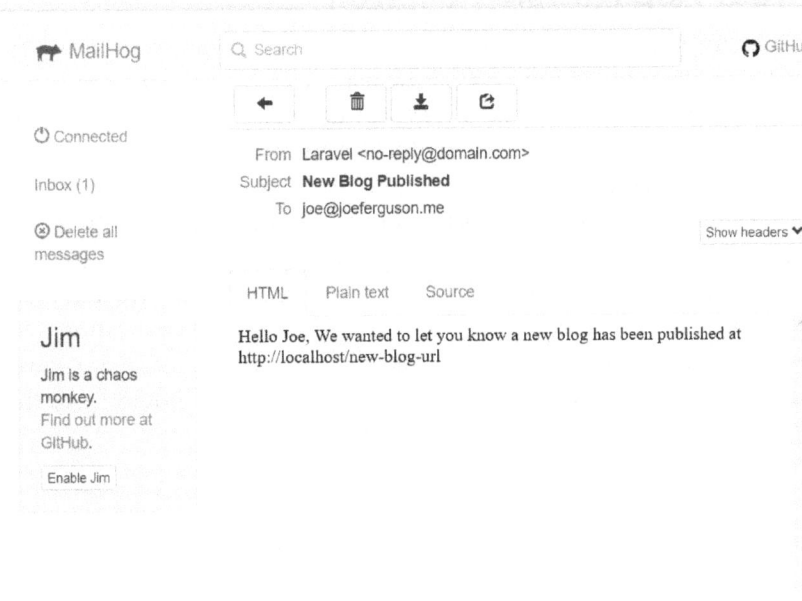

Figure 2.2.

Figure 2.3.

MailHog will also break down the email formatting and allow us to see HTML, Plain Text, or the raw source of the email (Figure 2.4) sent from our application.

MailHog allows us to test our application's email functionality in real-time as easy as checking any other function. Another fantastic feature of MailHog is Jim, the chaos money. You can enable Jim in MailHog to simulate mail server problems such as dropped connections, and slow or fast timeouts as sender rejection. Chaos monkey allows you to test exactly how your application will handle different mail failure

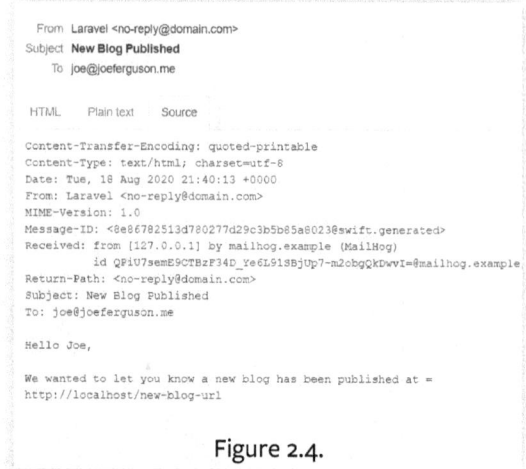

```
From    Laravel <no-reply@domain.com>
Subject New Blog Published
   To   joe@joeferguson.me

HTML       Plain text      Source

Content-Transfer-Encoding: quoted-printable
Content-Type: text/html; charset=utf-8
Date: Tue, 18 Aug 2020 21:40:13 +0000
From: Laravel <no-reply@domain.com>
MIME-Version: 1.0
Message-ID: <8e86782513d780277d29c3b5b85a8023@swift.generated>
Received: from [127.0.0.1] by mailhog.example (MailHog)
        id QPiU7semE9CTBzF34D_Ye6L91SBjUp7-m2obgQkDwvI=@mailhog.example
Return-Path: <no-reply@domain.com>
Subject: New Blog Published
To: joe@joeferguson.me

Hello Joe,

We wanted to let you know a new blog has been published at =
http://localhost/new-blog-url
```

Figure 2.4.

scenarios when connecting to STMP servers to send an email. MailHog also enables you to inspect the headers of the message to ensure any custom headers you may be using are preserved during the mail transport.

## Sharing Your Application Via ngrok

ngrok[4] is a lightweight application that creates public tunnels to your local development environment. While there are commercial ngrok plans which give you many more features, we can use the free tier to allow others to access our development environment in WSL from their systems. If you want to customize the domain ngrok assigns your project or need access to advanced features, the paid tiers are quite reasonable, considering you don't have to bug your IT team to open firewall ports for you. Never mind the security implications which come with open firewall ports and routing rules into someone's development environment. Most often, development environments are insecure since only trusted users access the application. There *are* certainly risks involved in opening your application to the public internet, especially since your environment is likely using a debug mode or environment. Be careful you don't leak any stack traces from errors to anyone who shouldn't see them. And don't forget to close a tunnel once you're done with it.

### Installation

We can install ngrok into our WSL distribution with the following commands to download, extract, and clean up our downloaded file. the Linux download URL found on https://ngrok.com/download

---

[4]   ngrok: *https://ngrok.com*

```
wget https://bin.equinox.io/c/4VmDzA7iaHb/ngrok-stable-linux-amd64.zip
unzip ngrok-stable-linux-amd64.zip -d /usr/local/bin
rm -rf ngrok-stable-linux-amd64.zip
```

## Creating a Tunnel

With ngrok installed into WSL, we're ready to share our blog project. We're using `blog.test` as our local development domain name. When we run ngrok, this is the domain we'll pass so that the tunnel from the internet routes traffic to the correct project in our WSL system.

Running the following command shows the output in Figure 2.5.

```
ngrok http blog.test
```

If your web server uses the `Host` header to route a virtual host request, you can tell ngrok to rewrite it like this:

```
ngrok http -host-header=blog.test blog.test
```

Notice that it includes a public, randomly-generated URL that expires when we close ngrok via control + C or when the session expires. Free sessions are limited to 8 hours.

```
halo@Rage:~/LinuxCode/blog    ×       halo@Rage:/etc/nginx/sites-ena    ×    +    ∨

ngrok by @inconshreveable

Session Status                online
Session Expires               7 hours, 57 minutes
Version                       2.3.35
Region                        United States (us)
Web Interface                 http://127.0.0.1:4040
Forwarding                    http://85c5846d8d5a.ngrok.io -> http://blog.test:80
Forwarding                    https://85c5846d8d5a.ngrok.io -> http://blog.test:80

Connections                   ttl       opn       rt1       rt5       p50       p90
                              0         0         0.00      0.00      0.00      0.00
```

Figure 2.5.

### Sharing Our Dev Site

Ngrok will create SSL and HTTP tunnels to our local site. The URL to share, in this example, is `http://85c5846d8d5a.ngrok.io`. If we open this in our browser (Figure 2.6), we see the same generic Laravel homepage we see when we browse `http://blog.test` on our local system. However, anyone with our ngrok URL can now see and use our application.

We can click "register", fill out the basic registration form, and submit to create our user account as in Figure 2.7. Ngrok shows you the HTTP requests in real-time in the console, and we can see our application has no idea it's not running locally.

### Inspecting Requests

Also included with ngrok is a web interface, shown in Figure 2.8, running on http://127.0.0.1:4040, which gives us deep introspection into the requests traveling across our tunnel.

We can see the POST request when I submitted the user registration form. We can also see the request was posted to the `/register` route in our application and also inspect the form values I submitted. Remember, development environments are often insecure, so you shouldn't use any email or password which should remain secret. Ngrok also allows you to replay these requests from the UI, which can be useful when working with webhooks or external APIs such as Stripe for payment processing.

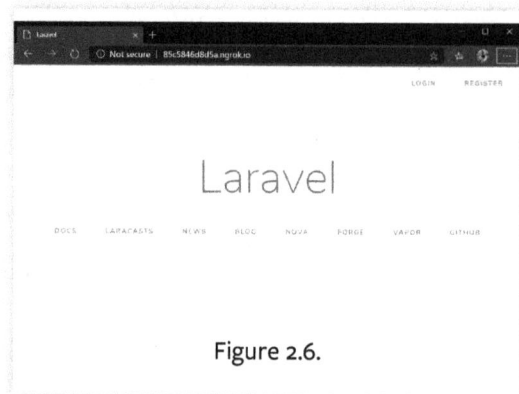

Figure 2.6.

Figure 2.7.

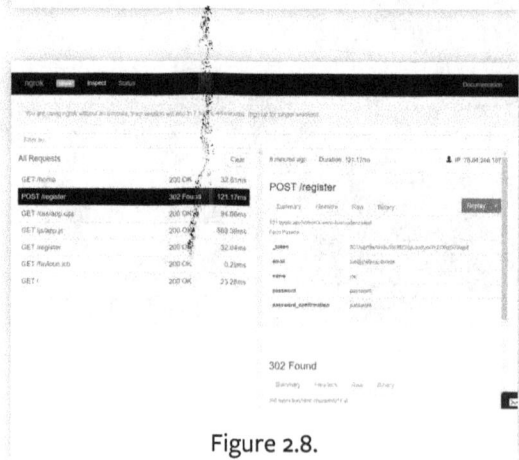

Figure 2.8.

When we're done sharing our application, use control + C in the ngrok window to close the tunnel. We're no longer sharing to anyone with our URL, and if we refresh our browser where we had registered our user, we'll see an error such as "Tunnel 811dc63d3074.ngrok.io not found".

We have scratched the surface on what ngrok can do. You can use different regions to share your application closer to your colleagues if you're not in North America. Ngrok also supports several different configuration options, which can be loaded from a configuration file instead of remembering a complicated command-line syntax.

## Step Debugging With Xdebug

Step debugging is one of the most popular ways to interactively pause the execution of your application and watch the runtime variables change as your code is executed line by line. You can set breakpoints in your code where Xdebug will pause execution and wait for you to instruct it to continue. This allows us to explore what our application is doing and verify what we expect to be happening is actually happening. Step debugging is also a great way to debug code written in an unfamiliar framework to visualize what the framework is doing and how it's interacting with your code. You'll often hear developers use the term "die and dump debugging" or "var dump and die" to describe placing var_dump($some_variable); exit() code around their application which will dump our the specified variable and exit the program. Step debugging can be considered the opposite style of debugging because you're able to pause execution and inspect any variable and the global application state.

Debugging PHP is sometimes an exercise in frustration for developers. Since PHP web applications typically have minimal execution periods, we have to configure Xdebug and our code editor to recognize our browser request and allow Xdebug to pause and step through its execution. The most common issue I have encountered with developers struggling to get Xdebug working in their project is configuration errors with their editor and ensuring the local files are correctly mapped to the URL being executed. Once we understand how the mapping of files needs to work and configure our editor to debug our project, we'll be on our way to step debugging.

### Installing Xdebug

If you followed last month's GitHub gist[5] to install PHP, you should already have Xdebug installed. If not, make sure you run the following before continuing.

```
sudo apt-get install php-xdebug
```

---

[5]   GitHub gist: http://phpa.me/github-svpernova09-bc441

We also need to double-check that the settings in /etc/php/7.4/mods-available/xdebug.ini look like this:

```
zend_extension=xdebug.so
xdebug.remote_enable=1
xdebug.remote_port=9000
xdebug.idekey=PHPSTORM
xdebug.remote_host=172.23.128.1
```

> You might be wondering why we're not using remote_autostart[6]. If you add xdebug.remote_autostart=1 to xdebug.ini, Xdebug will attempt to connect to the client on every request. This feature will negate the need to use the bookmarklets or browser plugins but may add latency to your HTTP requests.

You'll need to change 172.23.128.1 to whatever the IP WSL has assigned to /etc/resolv.conf as the nameserver. It is the IP address of WSL. Technically, WSL is a virtual machine, so it's not really localhost, even if other services appear to be. We need to add this remote host configuration option to Xdebug so that it knows how to connect back to our editor. Note this IP can and will change. This is one of the biggest pains I have with WSL, and my only solution is to write a script to check the IP and update it as needed. After we've made these changes make sure you restart PHP-FPM via:

```
sudo service php7.4-fpm restart
```

The configuration tells Xdebug to use port 9000 to communicate with our editor and allows us to enable Xdebug remotely. We'll cover the setup and configuration for both PhpStorm and Visual Studio Code editors. The configuration is similar for any editor, but based on my 100% unscientific guess: *most* PHP developers are using PhpStorm or VS Code.

## PhpStorm Configuration

To configure Xdebug with PhpStorm, open our project and navigate to the Run menu and select "Edit Configurations". Clicking the plus sign in the top left of the pane will display several options. We want to select "PHP Remote Debug," which creates a new PHP Remote Debug configuration. Don't be confused with *remote* while we're running this locally on our WSL distribution. Remote, in this case, is referring to the PHP connection that we're debugging, which is running behind a web server: NGINX and PHP-FPM.

---

[6]  remote_autostart: http://phpa.me/xdebug-remote-autostart

You may also need to explicitly allow Windows Firewall to permit Xdebug to talk to WSL by running the following command in an elevated Powershell prompt, which generates the output shown in Figure 2.9.

```
New-NetFirewallRule -DisplayName "WSL" -Direction Inbound \
  -InterfaceAlias "vEthernet (WSL)"  -Action All
```

You can find more information on the WSL Github[7].

We'll name our configuration "blog.test WSL" to indicate this is our blog project running in WSL. We want to enable "Filter debug connection by IDE key" so we can easily enable and disable Xdebug in individual browser windows. I use "PHPSTORM" as the IDE key because Jetbrains has made bookmarks[8] available that you can use to turn on and off debugging quickly for the current page in your browser. You'll want to take a few minutes and configure these in your browser. We'll need "Start Debugger" and "Stop Debugger" bookmarklets. Next, we need to configure the server running our application. Click on the ellipsis menu to the right of the server selection dropdown menu to open the "Servers" window. Clicking on the plus sign will create a new unnamed server and allow us to select a

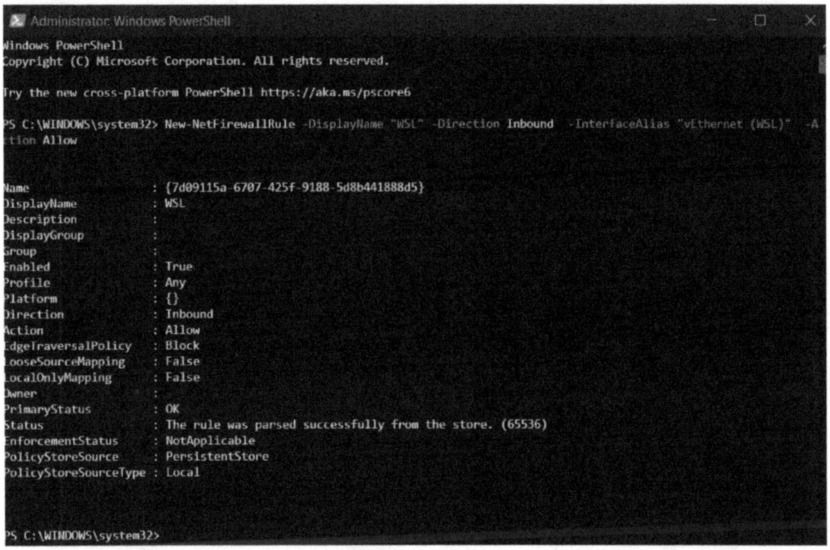

Figure 2.9.

---

[7] WSL Github: https://github.com/microsoft/WSL/issues/4585
[8] made bookmarks: https://www.jetbrains.com/phpstorm/marklets/

debugger and port. We'll name our server "blog.test WSL" and use `http://blog.test` as our Host. We can leave port 80 and Debugger set to Xdebug.

Now we're at the point where so many developers get frustrated. They forget to enable the "Use path mappings" option and configure their directories, which leads to Xdebug unable to connect properly. Path mappings are how PhpStorm and Xdebug match the files running in our editor as the same files running on the remote server, in WSL. We need to provide an absolute path on the server to where these files are. On my system, I have created the blog project in my WSL user's home directory. The full path being `/home/halo/LinuxCode/blog`. You can see our PHP Remote Debug configuration and our Server configuration in Figure 2.10.

Once you have filled out the absolute path, we can click on "OK" to close the "Servers" window and "OK" to close the Run/Debug Configurations window. This is all the configuration we need to do in PhpStorm. In the UI, we can now select "Start listening for PHP debug connections."

To save you time, use PHPstorms built-in validation for Xdebug configurations. See "Validate the Configuration of a Debugging Engine"[9].

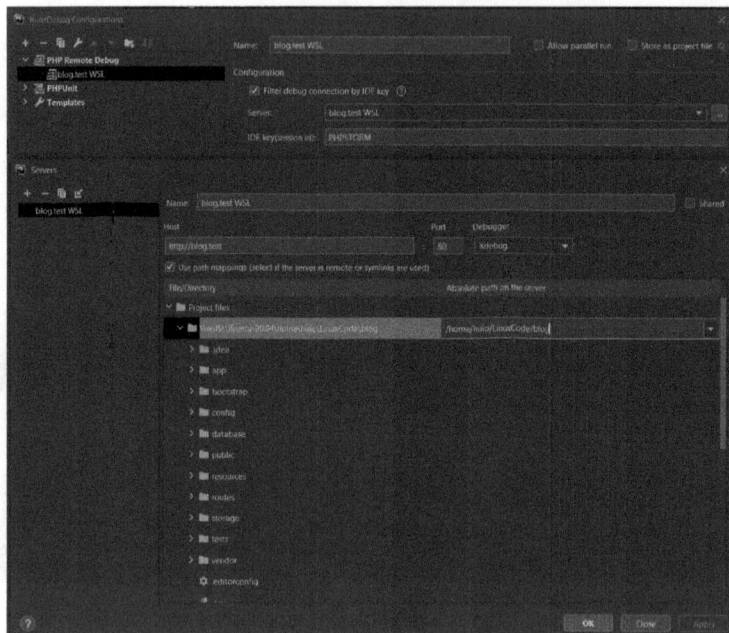

Figure 2.10.

---

[9]   "Validate the Configuration of a Debugging Engine": http://phpa.me/jetbrains-validate-debugging

# Configuring Visual Studio Code

To enable Xdebugging in VS Code, we need to install the PHP Debug extension[10] from Felix Becker. Once installed, we'll open the Run panel by clicking on the icon or using ctrl + shift + d keyboard shortcut. VS Code uses a `launch.json` file (Listing 2.3) to configure the launch targets. This step is similar to PhpStorm's Run configurations. Click on the "create a launch.json file" link to create a new file for us with two configurations: "Listen for Xdebug" and "Launch currently open script". We're only interested in the "Listen for Xdebug" configuration, and we'll add a `pathMappings` option to tell VS Code how to connect our paths similarly to how we configured PhpStorm.

Listing 2.3. .vscode/launch.json

```
1.  {
2.    "version": "0.2.0",
3.    "configurations": [
4.      {
5.        "name": "Listen for XDebug",
6.        "type": "php",
7.        "request": "launch",
8.        "port": 9000,
9.        "pathMappings": {
10.         "/home/halo/LinuxCode/blog": "${workspaceRoot}"
11.       }
12.     },
13.     {
14.       "name": "Launch currently open script",
15.       "type": "php",
16.       "request": "launch",
17.       "program": "${file}",
18.       "cwd": "${fileDirname}",
19.       "port": 9000
20.     }
21.   ]
22. }
```

Save our changes and then go back to the "Run" menu, and our configuration should show up. You'll see a button to click to select "Listen For Xdebug Connections."

---

[10] PHP Debug extension: *http://phpa.me/felixfbecker-php-debug*

## Step Debugging In Action

There are three ways you can trigger Xdebug from your browser. You can use bookmarks as PhpStorm provides, browser plugins, or GET parameters such as `?XDEBUG_SESSION_START=PHPSTORM`. I typically use the bookmarks or the GET parameter to do one-off or isolated debugging.

Opening the URL `http://blog.test/?XDEBUG_SESSION_START=PHPSTORM` triggers VS Code to pause at line 17 of our `routes/web.php` file because we set a breakpoint here. We can click the "Step Over" (F10 Keyboard Shortcut) icon in the top center toolbar to execute line 17 without going into the function itself. It queries the database for all users and returns a collection object of the results. After it runs, we see our `$users` variable on the left pane of VS Code, which I have expanded to show the attributes of a user I had previously registered (Figure 2.11).

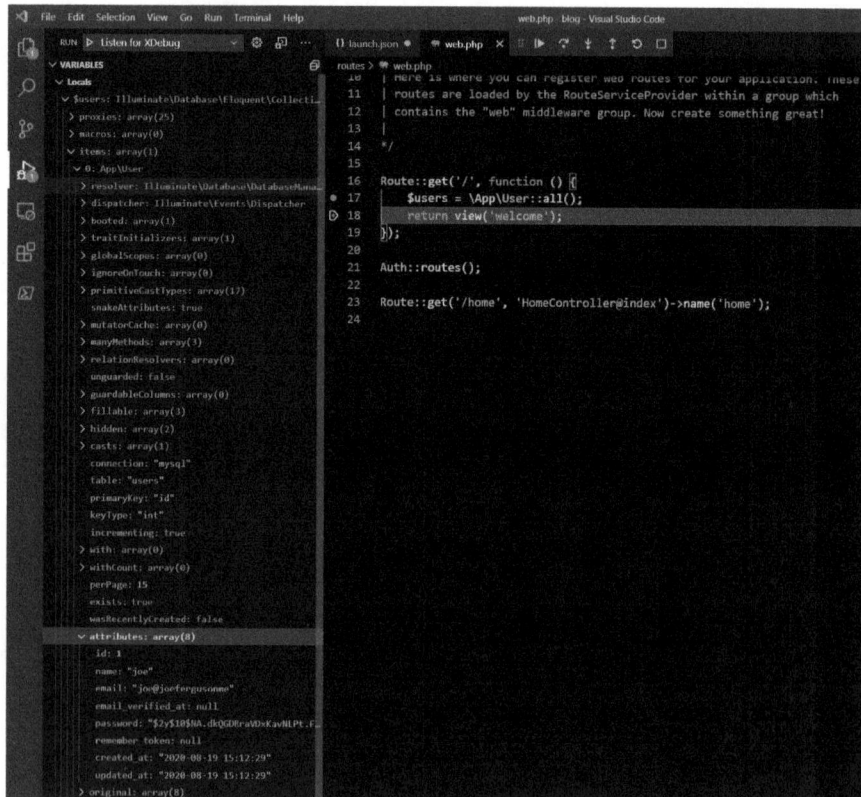

Figure 2.11.

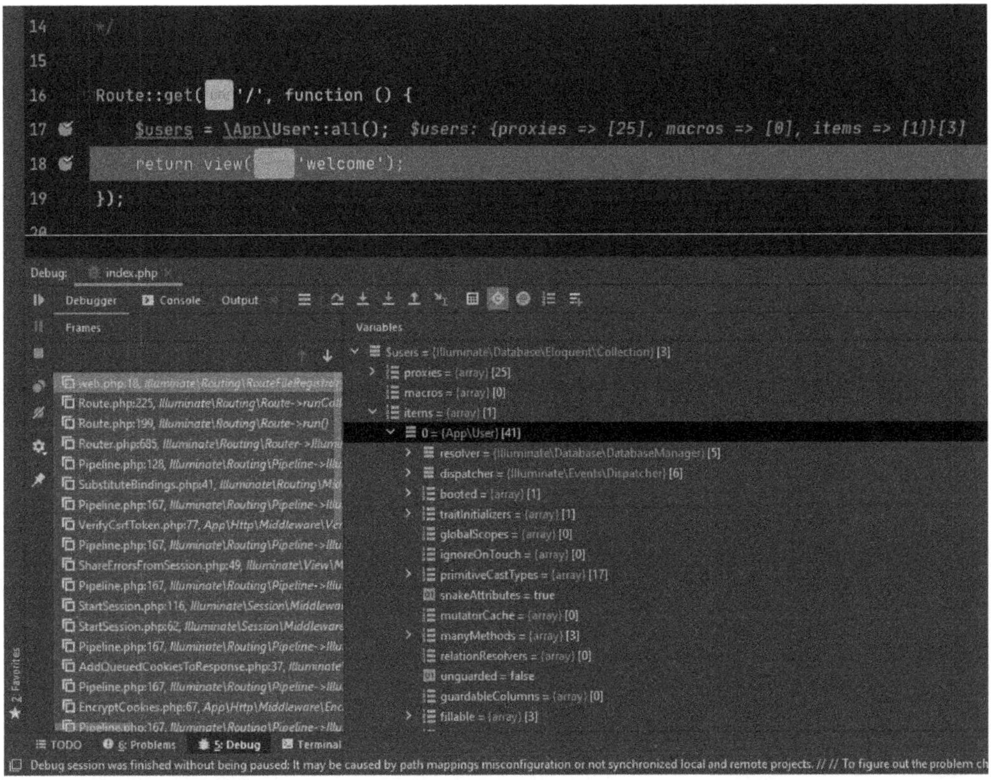

Figure 2.12.

The same request using PhpStorm shows us the debug UI as in Figure 2.12.

## Conclusion

Whatever editor you're using, I hope you check out how great WSL can be for Windows PHP development. There are some rough edges like having to find the WSL IP. However, Microsoft is committed to WSL for the long haul and had a lot of news to share[11] from their BUILD developer conference in May 2020.

---

[11] *news to share:* http://phpa.me/wsl-2020-summary

# Chapter

# 3

# PHP Development with Homestead in WSL

Homestead is a fantastic PHP development environment that provides many tools PHP developers have come to expect: NGINX and Apache support, easy access to multiple PHP versions, MySQL and PostgreSQL databases, and an easy "reset" method in case something goes wrong you can quickly get back to a known state. In thi chapter, we're going to explore the ongoing Homestead development to bring some of the polish and ease of use from Homestead to WSL.

## 3. PHP Development with Homestead in WSL

We've spent the past two chapters talking about Windows Subsystem for Linux (WSL) in Windows 10 and how to customize it to serve as a PHP development environment. While functional, our environment lacked a fair bit of polish. In the nearly four years that I've been working on and maintaining Laravel Homestead[1], I've spent much of that time adding functionality and polish to the Laravel focused Vagrant development environment.

We previously had to do a lot of work to build and provision our PHP environment. Using Homestead, we can leverage a longstanding project made for the latest PHP versions on Ubuntu which translates well to using it as your WSL Distribution.

# Benching Ruby

Homestead was originally written to work with Vagrant. This application abstracts working with virtual machines and acts as an API client to a hypervisor such as Virtualbox, VMware, etc. Since Vagrant is written in Ruby, Homestead utilizes a Ruby class to translate the Homestead.yaml configuration file users edit to add projects to the environment. Our Homestead Ruby class parses the configuration and runs different shell scripts to configure the Ubuntu 20.04 virtual machine as the user had specified. At its core, Homestead is a sprinkle of Ruby on top of a Bash script ice cream sundae. This design choice makes it possible to modify Homestead to work with WSL with some of the polish. While this first iteration isn't as much polish as you'd potentially expect, remember WSL is a relatively new technology. Our primary goals are to deliver PHP 7.4 and 7.3 via NGINX and PHP-FPM, and MySQL database access, without making our users write and configure their virtual hosts or manually create their databases.

For WSL, we need to replace the Homestead Ruby class which acts as a dispatcher for our provisioning shell scripts that, in turn, create our configuration files and ensure features are installed and enabled correctly for use. We can complete the initial configuration by running a single Bash script. However, we'll need more advanced parsing of the Homestead. yaml configuration file. We'll use Symonfy's Console[2] component to build PHP command-line tools to run our bash scripts once we've completed the initial configuration. Homestead already contains one of these commands for allowing you to install the development environment[3] directly into your application with Composer. So we'll be replacing our Ruby dispatching with PHP Classes to handle running our shell scripts to configure our environment.

---

[1]   Laravel Homestead: https://github.com/laravel/homestead
[2]   Console: https://symfony.com/doc/current/console.html
[3]   development environment: http://phpa.me/homestead-8-per-project

# Homestead Is Not Idempotent

Idempotence[4] is a way to describe operations that can be applied multiple times without changing the result past the initial execution. Common examples of idempotency you may have already experienced could be using HTTP Verbs such as GET, PUT, and DELETE. We consider them idempotent operations because they can be applied many times without changing the response outcome. Using GET, we want to fetch data from an endpoint such as `api/widgets/` which returns a list of all widgets without updating or affecting the widgets in any way. No matter how many times we call our endpoint, we'll always get a list of known widgets. When we use PUT to update a database record, we're taking a current state of the record's properties such as ID, name, and price and applying those properties to the database with a known identifier. If we replayed our PUT request repeatedly with the same identifier, the result would continue to come back the same, resulting in the PUT request being idempotent, not causing any side effects by multiple operations. A POST operation that submits a contact form wouldn't be idempotent because there may not be a unique identifier, such as an ID. As in, the application is only relaying a message from a comment box.

In the DevOps world, idempotency is most often used to describe provisioning tools such as Chef, Ansible, or Puppet. These tools are designed to be run repeatedly against the same systems to apply the desired state. The state comes from playbooks and cookbooks in Ansible and Chef systems, which describe what packages to install and how to configure them. This description includes deploying an application. The steps you take to deploy an application to production should be idempotent. You don't want to introduce unintended side effects to the desired state—your application running in production.

All of this talk about idempotency is to help you understand that we're *not* able to guarantee idempotency from Homestead scripts. Ansible playbooks and Chef cookbooks can ensure that because they programmatically check if a step was performed. If your playbook says to install the `php7.4-cli` package, the Ansible modules in charge of installing this application can check if it's already installed. If so, it can safely skip this step. Bash scripts lack the intelligent processing capabilities present in Ansible and other provisioning tools. While Homestead is *not* idempotent, it's crucial to understand how to get back to a known good state. With traditional Homestead usage on Vagrant, users can "reset" the virtual machine. With WSL, we need to have the ability to do the same thing: revert to a known good state.

---

[4]  Idempotence: *https://en.wikipedia.org/wiki/Idempotence*

## Starting A Fresh WSL Distribution

In case you've already been using WSL, you can export your current distribution by using the following commands to export it and remove it (You can re-import later via `wsl --import`).

```
wsl --export Ubuntu-20.04 Ubuntu-20.04.tar
wsl --terminate Ubuntu-20.04
wsl --unregister Ubuntu-20.04
```

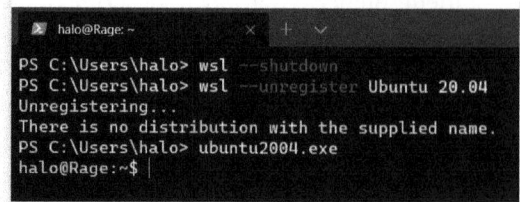

Figure 3.1.

If you don't currently have a Ubuntu-20.04 distribution installed, you can skip the export and unregister steps shown in Figure 3.1.

Creating a new copy of the Ubuntu-20.04 distribution can be done via Powershell CLI from the `ubuntu2004.exe`. Doing so makes a clean copy of the distribution ready to use. With a fresh distribution, we can launch "Ubuntu 20.04" from the Windows start menu. If you're using the newer Microsoft Terminal[5], you may already have a shortcut to the distri- bution in the menu as in Figure 3.2.

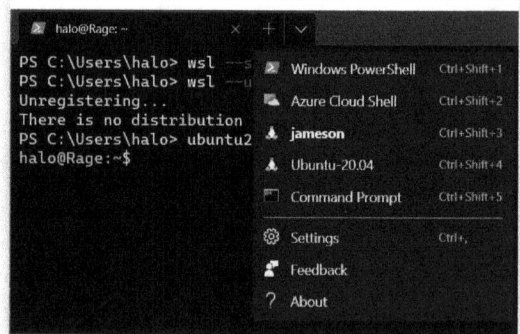

Figure 3.2.

Launching our new distribution from this menu should put us in our Windows user's home directory. See Figure 3.3.

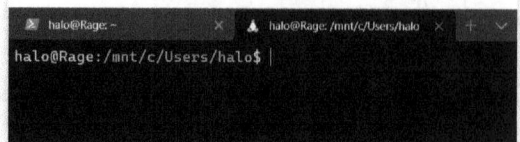

Figure 3.3.

## Homestead WSL Configuration

If you don't already have the Homestead repository cloned, go ahead and clone it:

```
$ git clone git@github.com:laravel/homestead.git
```

Once you have the Homestead repo, you don't need to worry about installing anything with Composer. Remember, our goal is for users to clone the Homestead repository and then run an initial provision or initialization script to bootstrap everything we'll need. We want to change the directory to our Homestead repo and then run:

---

[5]   newer Microsoft Terminal: http://phpa.me/ms-windows-terminal

```
sudo ./bin/wsl-init
```

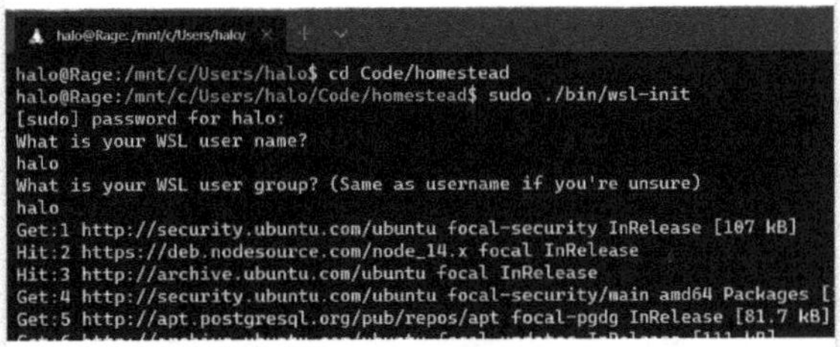

You'll see output similar to Figure 3.4.

The wsl-init[6] bash script is a trimmed down version of the same script used to build the Homestead base boxes for Vagrant. The init script asks you for your WSL username and group name. In *most* cases, your group name should be the same as your user

Figure 3.4.

name. If your group name is different, you would have changed it yourself. It's important to input these values correctly because Homestead configures services to run as this user in Ubuntu, vastly simplifying permissions.

> *Homestead is not for production and should not be used to configure systems exposed to the internet. Homestead is insecure by design as a developer tool.*

The very last thing the script does is run composer install and bash init.sh on the Homestead repository itself. As you can see in the screenshot (3.1), I already have the Homestead files in my folder, so it's asking me if I want to overwrite them. If this is the first time you've used Homestead, you won't see that output. You only need to run the wsl-init script if you recreate your WSL distribution.

The very last thing the script does is run composer install and bash init.sh on the Homestead repository itself. As you can see in the screenshot (Figure 3.5), I already have the Homestead files in my folder, so it's asking me if I want to overwrite them. If this is the first time you've used Homestead, you won't see that output. You only need to run the wsl-init script if you recreate your WSL distribution.

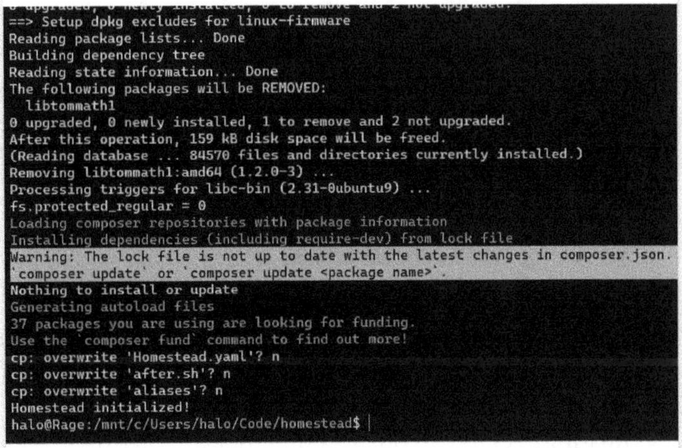

Figure 3.5.

---

[6]  wsl-init: http://phpa.me/blob-init-20-04

## Homestead Configuration

The Homestead.yaml configuration file is where you describe your *desired state* of the WSL system. As far as Homestead is concerned, it should be able to create virtual host configurations matched to local directories, create MySQL databases, and enable specified features. As previously mentioned, we'll be writing a Symfony Command class to act as our configuration parser and shell script dispatcher.

At the bottom of Homestead.yaml, we'll add a section named wsl_sites since the site configuration is somewhat different from the original Vagrant focused sites setting. My current configuration looks similar to:

```
wsl_sites:
    - map: paste.test
      to: /mnt/c/Users/halo/Code/isb-paste/public
    - map: vcdt.test
      to: /mnt/c/Users/halo/Code/vcdt/public
    - map: laminas.test
      to: /mnt/c/Users/halo/Code/laminas/public
```

With the above configuration we're mapping internal domain names to project locations on the filesystem, for example vcdt.test to /mnt/c/Users/halo/Code/vcdt/public which is C:\Users\halo\Code\vcdt\public on my Windows filesystem. You can mix and match projects from Windows paths or paths native to the WSL filesystem.

Remember, WSL is *still* somewhat new, and there are rough edges you may run across when it comes to filesystems between Windows and Linux in WSL usage. When encountering a weird permission issue or odd output from a command, I'll try flipping the files to the opposite filesystem to see if it was an issue of the WSL virtualization causing an unexpected result or output from a command. I've noticed NodeJS, in particular, can sometimes act differently when running in WSL.

### Creating Homestead Sites

The src/WslCreateSiteCommand.php file serves as our ./bin/homestead wsl:create-sites command to trigger Homestead to apply our site configuration from Homestead.yaml to WSL. We don't currently support *all* of the site options as we do on Vagrant. However, the basics are enough to get most modern PHP applications up and running. If there's a feature missing, feel free to open a pull request! You can also find me in the php[architect] Discord.

Before we can create sites, we'll need to create an array of arguments to pass to the Laravel site-type script /scripts/site-types/laravel.sh, which creates our virtual host files (Figure 3.6).

The $args array is where we apply our configuration with the defaults our script is expecting. Next, we create our command string on lines 77 & 78 by concatenating our expected arguments. Our $create_cmd value now is:

```
sudo bash scripts/site-types-laravel.sh paste.
test "mnt/c/Users/halo/Code/isb-paste/public" 80
443 7.4
```

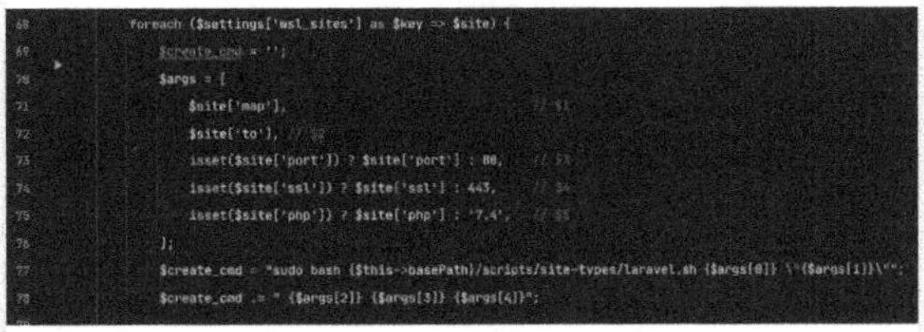

We'll build this command string (Figure 3.7) and execute it for each site found in our wsl_sites.

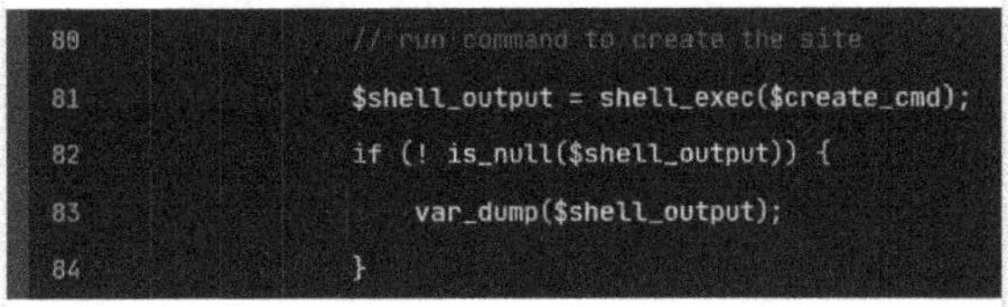

In the event something goes wrong, we're going to log the output of our command to $shell_output, then we hand our $create_cmd string off to trusty shell_exec() which executes our command and *will* block our PHP application while it runs. Most often, the output should be null or trivial confirmation messages. We only care about this output when it contains a stack trace or large error messages.

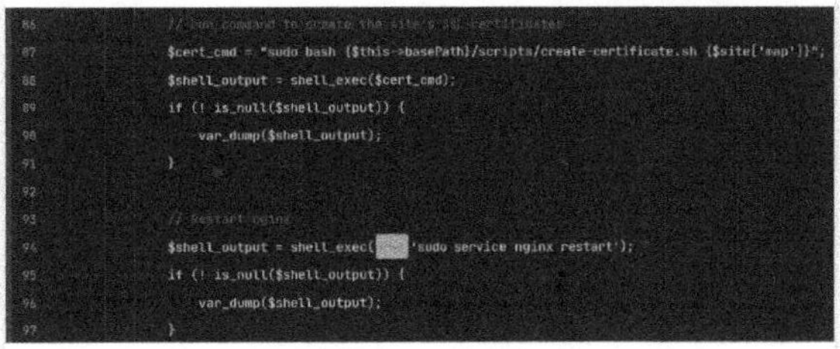

With our virtual host configuration now created, we need to make our certificates via scripts/create-certificate.sh. This script creates a basic self-signed certificate so you can test and verify SSL works with your application, as shown in Figure 3.8.

Lastly, we'll restart NGINX. We do this every time we create a site in case there's a configuration problem—it is easier to spot *which* site has the error. To execute our WslCreateSiteCommand we'll run ./bin/home-stead wsl:create-sites as in Figure 3.9.

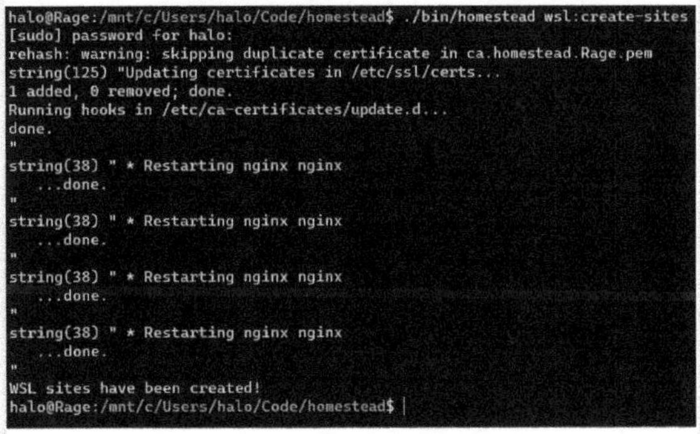

Figure 3.6.

Figure 3.7.

Figure 3.8.

Figure 3.9.

Our output looks normal, and there are no stack traces or error messages. We can inspect our virtual host file. See Figure 3.10.

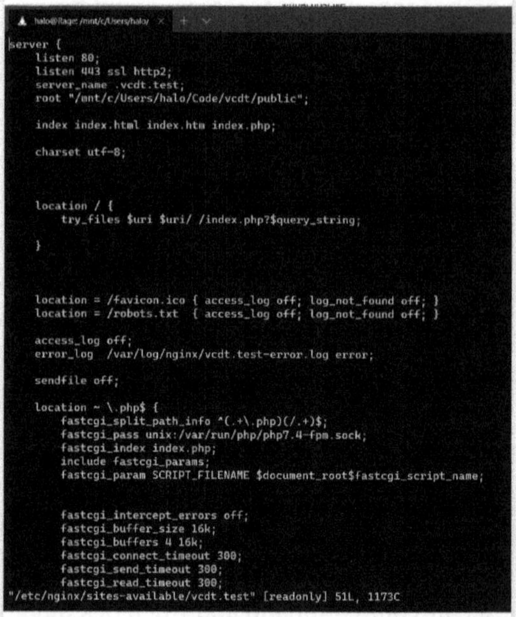

## Creating Databases

Our next command creates our MySQL databases found in the databases section of `Homestead.yaml`. At the moment, we're merely creating MySQL databases. Post-greSQL databases support requires further development. The `src/WslCreateDatabaseC-ommand.php` code loops over each database specified and ensures it's created if it doesn't already exist. It's important to note this is not a destructive action and is *idempotent*. You can run the command multiple times, and the same databases exists after the first run as the fifteenth run.

Figure 3.10.

From `Homestead.yaml`:

```
databases:
    - homestead
    - vcdt
    - laminas
```

Our `WslCreateDatabaseCommand` class is shown in Figure 3.11.

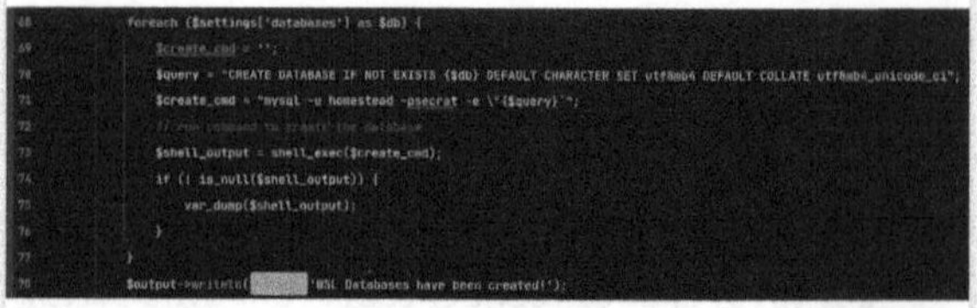

Figure 3.11.

Running our command creates any database if it is missing from the list and produces output shown in Figure 3.12.

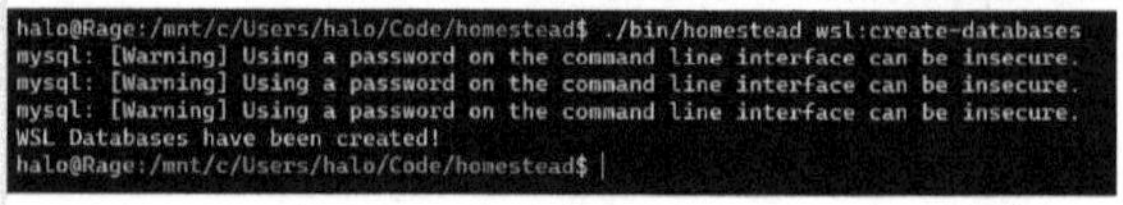

Again, we'll see some extraneous output warning that using our password on the command line can be insecure. Since we're in a development environment, we're not worried about command-line password security.

Figure 3.12.

If you need more access to your databases, you can configure applications like MySQL Workbench[7] to connect to the WSL MySQL server as in Figure 3.13.

## Something Went Wrong!

If something goes wrong or you are just ready to trash Homestead, you can delete the WSL distribution by unregistering it.

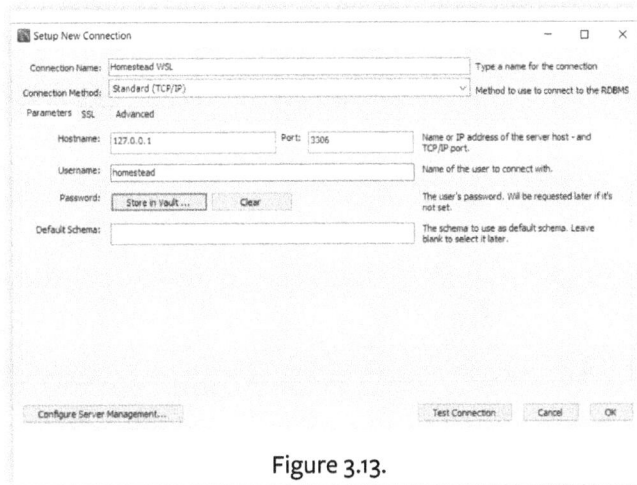

Figure 3.13.

> Before you unregister a WSL version, it is essential to remember you will lose anything in the Linux filesystem. This reason is why I use paths to my code on the Windows side of the filesystem. It allows me to quickly reload WSL distributions without losing my files. Although I lose my database contents, it's not an issue since I always seed development databases from database seeders or SQL backups.

When you're ready to nuke the WSL distribution:

```
wsl --unregister Ubuntu-20.04
```

## Some Polish, But More Needed

Admittedly, Homestead on WSL lacks the polish and features of the Vagrant experience. Still, if building this kind of tooling interests you, jump into GitHub and let's discuss how to make Homestead better. Hopefully, this encourages Windows users to test drive the compelling features WSL brings with native Linux.

Now that you have a fresh ready to use Homestead development environment in WSL, make sure you check out "The Workshop: Mail, Ngrok, and Xdebug in WSL," (see Related Reading). The Mailhog and Ngrok sections have already been done for you via wsl-init. You have a PHP 7.3 and 7.4 system ready for development.

---

[7]  MySQL Workbench: https://www.mysql.com/products/workbench/

# Chapter

# 4

# GUI Applications in WSL with X Server

We've spent the past few chapter discussing and demonstrating how to use WSL in your PHP development workflow as a better alternative to Virtual Machines by running native Linux on Windows 10. This month we're going to dive into an unsupported (by Microsoft) territory and cover how to and why we may run GUI applications in WSL distributions.

# 4. GUI Applications in WSL with X Server

At the time of this writing, Microsoft does not yet support running GUI applications in WSL, but it *is* coming as stated in a September 22nd, 2020 blog post[1]

> *"GUI app support in WSL is becoming a reality! We are getting closer to an initial preview and happy to announce a preview release for Windows Insiders within the next couple of months."*

Despite this, you can run some GUI applications on Windows 10 Pro Version 20H2, build 19042.572, or newer. If you're using an older version of Windows, your mileage may vary.

These days cross-platform applications are quite common thanks to Electron[2] where applications can enjoy a consistent execution on Windows, macOS, and Linux. Why would we want to run GUI applications in WSL? What if we don't have native or cross-platform options? Apart from the geek credibility of running an X server on Windows, the main benefit I have found is bypassing some of the filesystem latency issues WSL inherent between Windows and Linux filesystems.

One of the main differences between WSL versions 1 and 2[3] comes down to performance across OS file systems. Microsoft's recommendation for WSL 2 usage is to keep files being used by WSL in the Linux filesystem while keeping files used by Powershell on the Windows filesystem. Because WSL 2 implements full system call compatibility with Linux and a complete Linux kernel, filesystem operations are virtualized between WSL and Windows as files are accessed. If we create a new Laravel application via Composer in WSL on our Windows folder, it takes longer than if we run the same command on the WSL filesystem. We can compare the differences by first running the following in WSL on our Windows filesystem mounted at /mnt/c.

```
composer create-project --prefer-dist laravel/laravel WindowsLaravel
```

On my machine, it takes 6:29! Even pulling all of the packages from my local cache, this took a really long time (see Figure 4.1 and 4.2)

Figure 4.2.

---

[1]   September 22nd, 2020 blog post:
      http://phpa.me/ms-new-wsl-sept-2020
[2]   Electron: https://www.electronjs.org
[3]   differences between WSL versions 1 and 2:
      http://phpa.me/wsl-compare-versions

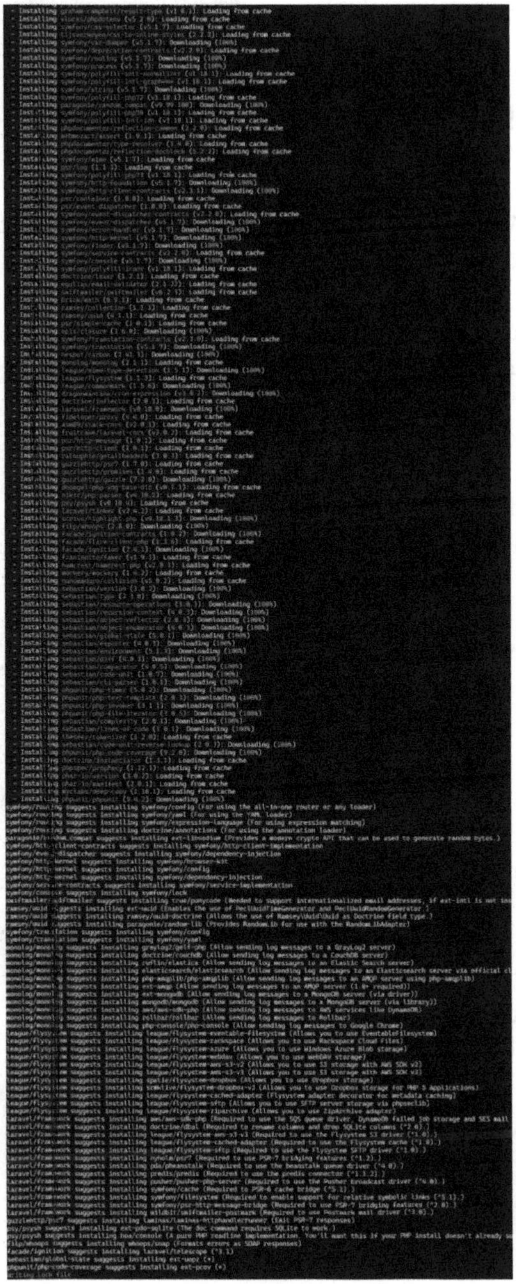

Figure 4.1.

Switching over to the WSL filesystem, we'll run the command again. You'll see something like Figure 4.3 and 4.4.

This time, we created our project from cache files in 11.552 seconds—quite a bit faster compared to the nearly six and a half minutes it took on our Windows filesystem. This is a -96.92% (390 seconds - 12 = 378 / 390 * 100) decrease in execution time of simply installing our packages. Keep this in mind when you run `php -S localhost:8000` to spin up a local server on your Windows filesystem. PHP's ability to read your files and execute them will also be subjected to this filesystem overhead. In our use cases, PHP is always being run **from** WSL, which is `/usr/bin/php` or whatever the Ubuntu default. If you run PHP on files on your Windows folders, you double dip the performance penalty.

Now, we understand why we want to focus on using our files in the filesystem in which we're operating on them. If you've tried to open a project from your WSL filesystem in PhpStorm running in Windows this is the exact filesystem latency you'd see. It's equivalent to editing files on a network share or volume. PhpStorm might even warn you about not being able to start file watchers because the folder is on a network.

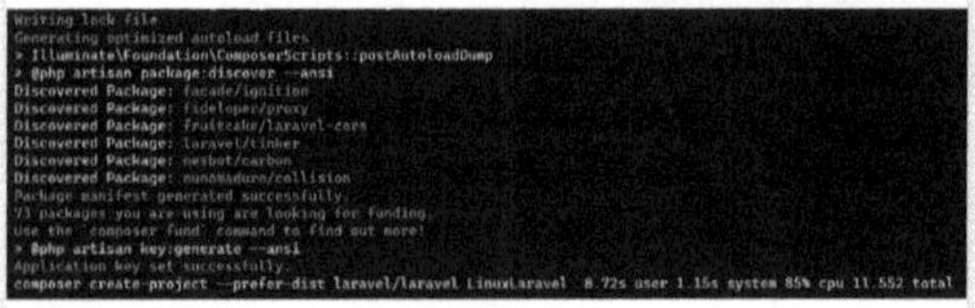

Figure 4.4.

Figure 4.3.

# X Server Options

This filesystem performance penalty led me to experiment with GUI applications in WSL, and I was thankful to find I wasn't the only one[4] interested in the idea. The X Window System[5] (X11, or simply X) is a windowing system for displays on Unix-like operating systems. X is the backend server that graphical interface clients can use to display windows. If you've used Desktop Linux distributions such as Ubuntu or Fedora, you've likely used Gnome or KDE desktop environments, which run on an X server. X is a backend service like any other. However, Windows 10 does not include an X server. We need to install an X server in Windows so that our WSL system can run graphical applications and connect to display those windows alongside our running Windows environment. There is a handful of X servers for Windows applications out there, but we'll cover two specific ones here: VcXsrv[6] and X410[7]. VcXsrv is free, while X410 is a paid product you can purchase in the Microsoft Store. These are the two most frequently used packages among WSL users based on stack overflow posts and blogs.

VcXsrv is the native X server packages compiled with Visual C++ 2012 Express Edition. It brings hardware acceleration to the X server, which the default X server on Windows does not support.

> We'll focus on VcXsrv, but I haven't used VcXsrv for very long. I moved on to using X410 primarily since it's a modified version of the X server codebase. Be aware that it does not support older Windows versions. However, the application is tuned and developed specifically for Windows 10. X410 usually costs $49.99, but I bought it for $9.99 during a "Save $40" sale via the Microsoft Store. I was happy to spend $10 to support the project. As I write, the sale is still going on—but might be over when you read this. You don't have to start with X410. VcXsrv will support most things until Microsoft directly provides official and better support.

After installing VcXsrv, we can launch it from the Windows menu, and we are greeted with a Display Settings window as in Figure 4.5.

---

[4]   only one: *http://phpa.me/sirredbeard-x-servers*
[5]   X Window System: *https://en.wikipedia.org/wiki/X_Window_System*
[6]   VcXsrv: *https://sourceforge.net/projects/vcxsrv/*
[7]   X410: *https://x410.dev*

X servers have two different modes of operation. You can either have multiple windows where each of your GUI applications launches in separate windows or have one large window containing all of the windows. Since I'm not running full desktop packages like Gnome or KDE, I prefer to have multiple windows.

The next question is how to start clients. We'll leave the default "Start no client" (see Figure 4.6).

We'll also leave the defaults on the Extra Settings as in Figure 4.7.

Now we're ready to save our configuration for later usage (Figure 4.8).

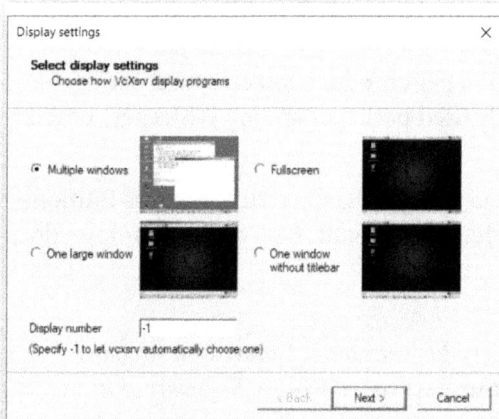

Figure 4.5.

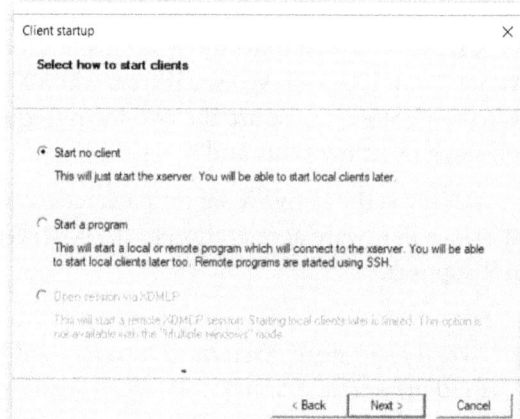

Figure 4.6.

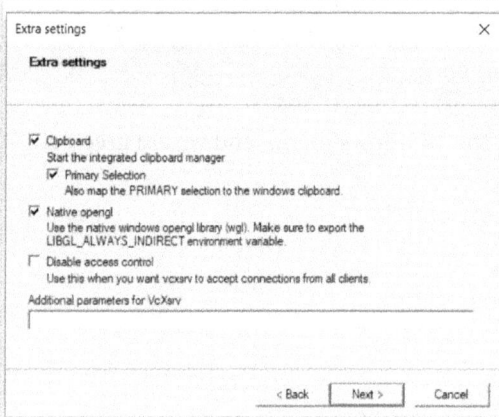

Figure 4.7.

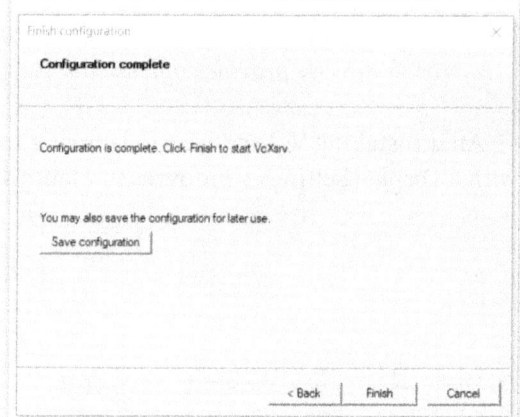

Figure 4.8.

Clicking finish will run our X server, and we should have an icon in the system tray as in Figure 4.9.

You can install X410 directly from the Microsoft Store as well as launch it from there or from the Windows menu. The configuration is much simpler than VcXsrv. Right-click on the white X410 logo in the system tray to open the menu shown in Figure 4.10.

I've selected the "Windowed Apps" setting to get multiple windows, and we also need to select "Allow Public Access." It allows WSL clients to connect to the X server running on Windows.

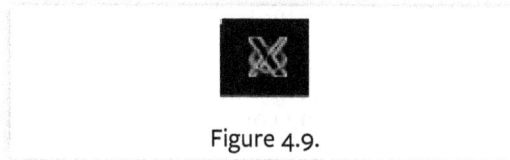

Figure 4.9.

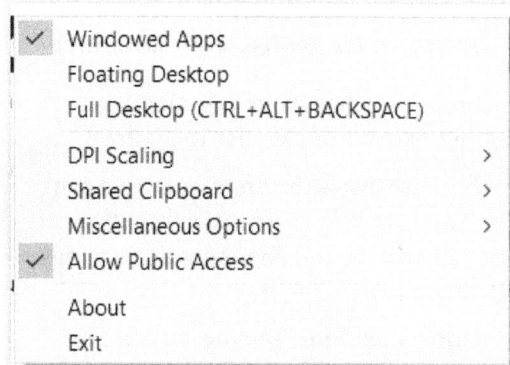

Figure 4.10.

## Configuring WSL

Now that we have our Windows X Server installed and running, we need to configure our WSL distribution to know where our "display" is. On normal Linux systems, this is typically 0.0.0.0:0.0. Because WSL has its own IP address, we need to tell our WSL console to get the IP of WSL and use that for our $DISPLAY environment variable. This way, whenever we open our WSL terminal, we automatically have it set. You'll want to add (all on one line) the following to ~/.bashrc or, in my case, since I'm using Zsh, ~/.zshrc:

```
# X11 WSL
export DISPLAY=$(cat /etc/resolv.conf | grep nameserver | awk '{print $2; exit;}'):0.0
```

We can check the value is set correctly by printing the $DISPLAY variable. It should contain an IP address and 0.0:

```
$ print $DISPLAY
172.30.224.1:0.0
```

We're done with X server configuration! Now that we've saved our environment variable to our WSL terminal, we must remember to start our X Server before starting any GUI Linux applications. Next up, we need to install some clients. We'll begin by installing PhpStorm 2020.2.3 from JetBrains with the following command.

```
wget https://download.jetbrains.com/webide/PhpStorm-2020.2.3.tar.gz
```

You'll get output similar to Figure 4.11.

Use the following command to extract the contents and launch PhpStorm.

```
tar -zxvf PhpStorm-2020.2.3.tar.gz
./PhpStorm-202.7660.42/bin/phpstorm.sh
```

Once launched, your command line should have output similar to Figure 4.12.

Because this is the first time we've run PhpStorm in WSL, we must accept the user agreement and configure our settings (Figure 4.13).

Congratulations, You're running the Linux version of PhpStorm via Windows Subsystem for Linux on Windows 10—without the filesystem performance penalty! Figure 4.14 is a screenshot from my system.

Figure 4.11.

Figure 4.12.

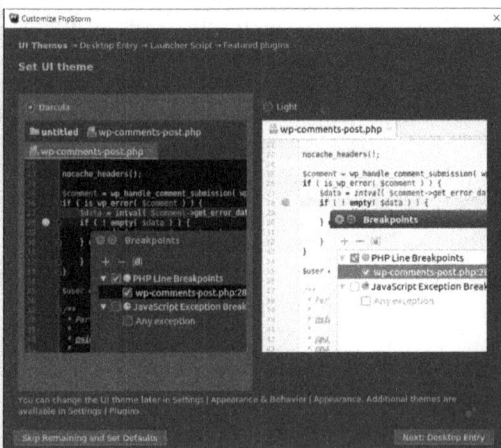

Figure 4.13.

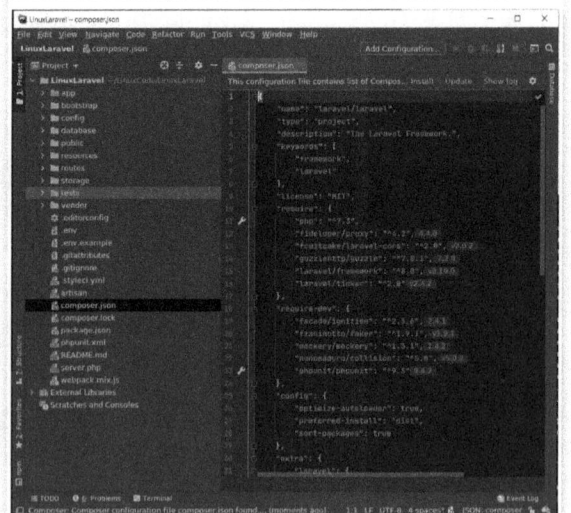

Figure 4.14.

What's that noise going on in the terminal (Figure 4.15)?! You might have noticed since we ran the PhpStorm binary script directly that the terminal fills up with output logs from the process. Worse, if you press Control + C in that terminal, you'll kill the process, and the PhpStorm window will disappear.

Figure 4.15.

If we close our WSL terminal, all of the running processes will also be closed. Here is where the GUI experience has its first pain point: closing terminals without accidentally closing running GUI windows. My primary workaround for this is to keep two WSL terminal tabs open. I use the Windows Terminal Preview[8], which allows me to keep WSL, Powershell, and Command Prompt shells running in the same window. I have one WSL tab designated for GUI apps. Any applications—such as PhpStorm, Firefox, Gitkraken, etc.— that I launch, I run from that shell. I have to remember not to close that window unless I'm sure I'm ready to terminate all those other processes as well.

Another way around this would be to install a lightweight display manager and use its taskbar to hold your Linux GUI applications in a macOS-like dock. We can do this with XFCE by running the following commands:

```
sudo apt install xfce4 xfce4-terminal
```

It installs several packages that we won't need and should remove since we're running in WSL:

```
sudo apt purge xfce4-power-manager xscreensaver gnome-screensaver light-locker
```

Next we'll need to only start up the XFCE components we really want:

```
xfsettingsd --sm-client-disable; xfce4-panel --sm-client-disable --disable-wm-check &
```

Now we have launched our panel. You'll likely want to unlock and move it somewhere more suitable, as shown in Figure 4.16.

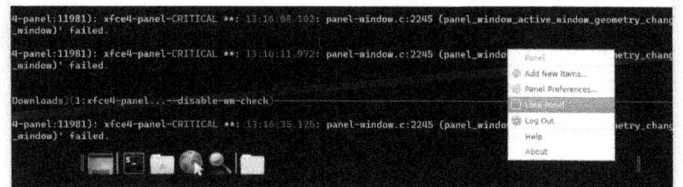

Figure 4.16.

---

[8] *Windows Terminal Preview:*
   *http://phpa.me/windows-terminal-preview*

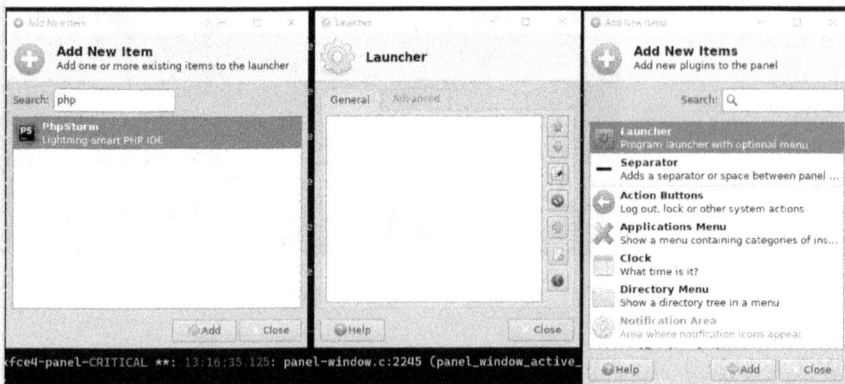

Figure 4.17.

Figure 4.18.

Feel free to move the panel wherever you prefer. You can right-click on the panel and click Panel Preferences to change the appearance. I changed mine to be vertical and moved it to the top right corner of my display, where I also have the Windows taskbar. Right-clicking on the panel and selecting Panel -> "Add new items" opens the menu to allow us to add a new Launcher, which we'll select PhpStorm from so we can add it to our dock. See Figure 4.17.

You can add as many launchers as you'd like or group applications into "folders." In Figure 4.18, I've added PhpStorm and Firefox to my bar.

You might have noticed we haven't solved our problem of "closing our WSL terminal closes our Linux application Windows". I prefer to continue using a hybrid "keep a tab open for GUI apps," which is essentially my XFCE panel to serve as a Linux application launcher.

If you prefer VS Code to PhpStorm we can install it via the following (watch the line wrapping):

```
wget -qO- https://packages.microsoft.com/keys/microsoft.asc | \
 gpg --dearmor > packages.microsoft.gpg
sudo install -o root -g root -m 644 packages.microsoft.gpg /etc/apt/trusted.gpg.d/
sudo sh -c 'echo "deb [arch=amd64 signed-by=/etc/apt/trusted.gpg.d/packages.microsoft.
gpg] https://packages.microsoft.com/repos/vscode stable main" > /etc/apt/sources.list.d/
vscode.list'
sudo apt-get update
sudo apt-get install code
```

Now, we can right-click on our panel, add a new launcher pointed at Code, and run VS Code, as shown in Figure 4.19.

Initially, I chased down the idea of getting GUI applications running in WSL because I enjoy using Gitkraken[9] as a GUI Git application. While it isn't free, it is a great tool that helps me make small commits and other quick tasks even faster than I can via the command line, as you can see in Figure 4.20.

If you want even tighter coupling of your Linux application launchers and your native Windows taskbar, I highly recommend X410's cookbook[10]. I'm not going to this extreme because I'm delighted with how my XFCE panel is working out, which is an idea I got from their cookbook. I'm also hoping Microsoft has something neat up their sleeve for how to do all of this "officially" in future versions of WSL and Windows 10.

What about the floating desktop mode? We can stop all of our X clients and change our mode to floating desktop to

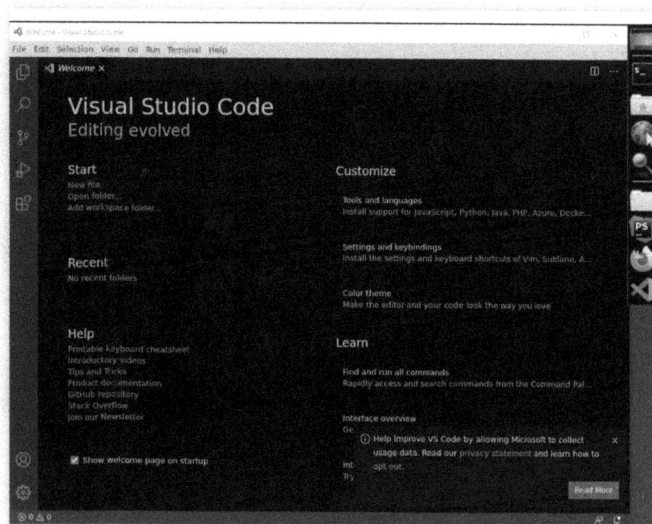

Figure 4.19.

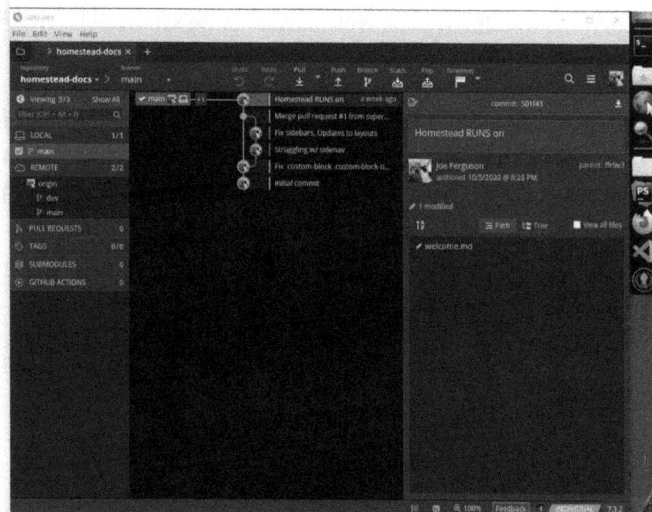

Figure 4.20.

[9]  Gitkraken: https://www.gitkraken.com
[10] X410's cookbook: http://phpa.me/x410-pin-linux

see the differences. Restarting our xterm panel, it will appear in this main window, as in Figure 4.21.

Any application we launch will take over this window completely. This behavior is useful if you're only ever going to run one application. The floating window feature fits with my workflow more comfortable. But I still have to remember to keep that WSL tab open.

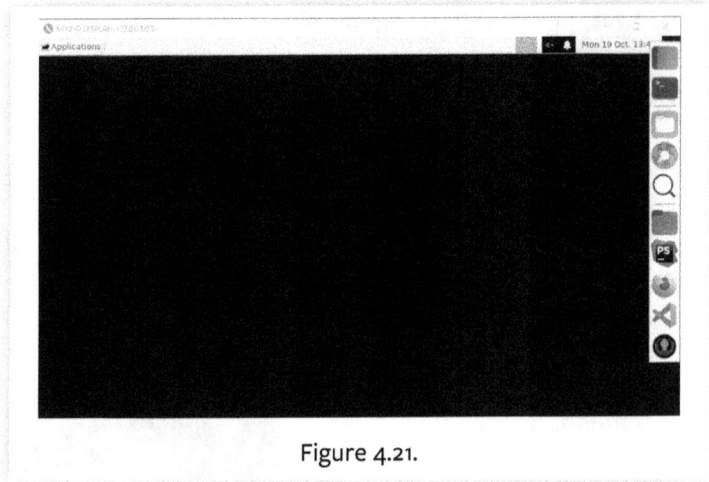

Figure 4.21.

There are two last things to leave you with on your GUI journey. Remember, now your code editor is running *inside* WSL; you'll need to reference paths using forward slashes starting from your /home/WSLUSERNAME/ path. Usually, you'd use something like C:\Users\Username\. The last thing is to keep regular backups. WSL is stable, but using unsupported things can lead to issues and potential data loss. Since all of our Linux running applications and code are now in our Linux filesystem, it's hard to include in our backup strategies. I regularly keep a snapshot of my WSL filesystem (which is included in my offsite backups) so that I can quickly roll back and only miss a day or two of changes. Most of the time, projects are stored in version control but keep this in mind when working with unversioned files inside WSL.

# Index

# php[architect] Books

The php[architect] series of books cover topics relevant to modern PHP programming. We offer our books in both print and digital formats. Print copy price includes free shipping to the US. Books sold digitally are available to you DRM-free in PDF, ePub, or Mobi formats for viewing on any device that supports these.

To view the complete selection of books and order a copy of your own, please visit: http://phparch.com/books/.

- **WordPress Development in Depth**
  By Peter MacIntyre, Savio Resende
  ISBN: 978-1940111834

- **The Grumpy Programmer's Guide To Testing PHP Applications (print edition)**
  By Chris Hartjes
  ISBN: 978-1940111797

- **The Fizz Buzz Fix: Secrets to Thinking Like an Experienced Software Developer**
  By Edward Barnard
  ISBN: 978-1940111759

- **The Dev Lead Trenches: Lessons for Managing Developers**
  By Chris Tankersley
  ISBN: 978-1940111711

- **Web Scraping with PHP, 2nd Edition**
  By Matthew Turland
  ISBN: 978-1940111674

- **Security Principles for PHP Applications**
  By Eric Mann
  ISBN: 978-1940111612

- **Docker for Developers, 2nd Edition**
  By Chris Tankersley
  ISBN: 978-1940111568 (Print edition)

- **What's Next? Professional Development Advice**
  Edited by Oscar Merida
  ISBN: 978-1940111513

- **Functional Programing in PHP, 2nd Edition**
  By: Simon Holywell
  ISBN: 978-1940111469

- **Web Security 2016**
  Edited by Oscar Merida
  ISBN: 978-1940111414

- **Integrating Web Services
  with OAuth and PHP**
  By Matthew Frost
  ISBN: 978-1940111261

- **Zend Framework 1 to 2
  Migration Guide**
  By Bart McLeod
  ISBN: 978-1940111216

- **XML Parsing with PHP**
  By John M. Stokes
  ISBN: 978-1940111162

- **Zend PHP 5 Certification
  Study Guide, Third Edition**
  By Davey Shafik with Ben Ramsey
  ISBN: 978-1940111100

- **Mastering the SPL Library**
  By Joshua Thijssen
  ISBN: 978-1940111001

# Feedback and Updates

Please let us know what you thought of this book! What did you enjoy? What was confusing or could have been improved? Did you find errata? Any feedback and thoughts you have regarding this book will help us improve a future edition.

## From the Publisher

To keep in touch and be notified about future editions to this book, visit http://phparch.com and sign up for our (low-volume) mailing list.

You can also follow us on twitter, @phparch, as well as on facebook: https://facebook.com/phparch/

www.ingramcontent.com/pod-product-compliance
Lightning Source LLC
Chambersburg PA
CBHW061618210326
41520CB00041B/7494